Kansas

by Rebecca Olien

Consultant:
Roy Bird
Consultant
Kansas State Library

Capstone press
Mankato, Minnesota

Capstone Press
151 Good Counsel Drive • P.O. Box 669 • Mankato, Minnesota 56002
www.capstonepress.com

Library of Congress Cataloging-in-Publication Data
Olien, Rebecca.
    Kansas / by Rebecca Olien.
    p. cm.—(Land of liberty)
    Summary: An introduction to the geography, history, government, politics,
economy, resources, people, and culture of Kansas, including maps, charts, and
a recipe.
    Includes bibliographical references and index.
    ISBN-13: 978-0-7368-1584-0 (library binding)
    ISBN-10: 0-7368-1584-8 (library binding)
    1. Kansas—Juvenile literature. [1. Kansas.] I. Title. II. Series.
F681.3.O44 2003
978.1—dc21   2002010813

Editorial Credits

Angela Kaelberer, editor; Jennifer Schonborn, series and book designer;
    Angi Gahler, illustrator; Karrey Tweten, photo researcher; Eric Kudalis,
    product planning editor

Photo Credits

Cover images: Tallgrass Prairie National Preserve, Steve Mulligan;
    Kansas wheat field, Corbis

Capstone Press/Gary Sundermeyer, 54; Corbis/Minnesota Historical Society, 36;
Corbis/Bettmann, 42; Corbis/Philip Gould, 48; Digital Stock, 1; Fort
Leavenworth Official U.S. Army photograph/Don Middleton, 44; Harland J.
Schuster, 22–23, 45; Hulton Archive by Getty Images, 18, 20, 28, 30; Hulton
Archive by Getty Images/Wizard of Oz Studio: MGM Director: Victor Fleming,
50; Index Stock Imagery/Aneal Vohra, 46; James E. Gerholdt, 14; Kansas State
Historical Society, 24, 27, 58; Kansas Travel and Tourism Development, 32, 38,
56; One Mile Up, Inc., 55 (both); Panoramic Images/David Lawrence, 40–41;
Panoramic Images, 52–53; Robert McCaw, 57 (both); Steve Mulligan, 4, 8, 12–13,
16, 63; U.S. Postal Service, 59; Wichita State University Libraries, 15

Artistic Effects

Corbis, Digital Stock, Kansas Travel and Tourism Development

Table of Contents

Keyhole Arch offers a view of another rock form at Monument Rocks National Monument.

4

Chapter 1

About Kansas

Most of the flat western Kansas land stretches miles in every direction. But the land is different 30 miles (48 kilometers) south of Oakley, Kansas. Here, huge forms of soft chalk rock rise 60 feet (18 meters) above the plains.

Monument Rocks National Monument formed from an ocean that once covered western Kansas. About 80 million years ago, that ocean dried up. A layer of wet chalk was left behind. Winds dried the chalk, and it formed into rock layers. Over millions of years, the wind wore away the soft rock. The wind carved it into forms that look like towers, arches, and keyholes.

Monument Rocks is only one famous rock form in Kansas. Castle Rock is located east of Monument Rocks. This 60-foot (18-meter) chalk rock looks like a castle's tower. Rock City is in eastern Kansas near Minneapolis. About 200 huge sandstone rocks cover the landscape. Some of these stones are the size of houses.

Sunflower State

Kansas is nicknamed the Sunflower State. Native sunflowers grow wild in fields and along roads. Kansas chose the native sunflower as its official state flower in 1903.

Kansas is located in the center of the connected 48 states. The exact center of the 48 states is 1 mile (1.6 kilometers) north of Lebanon in north-central Kansas.

Kansas is a rectangle shape. Each side borders another state. Missouri lies to the east. Nebraska borders Kansas on the north, Colorado lies to the west, and Oklahoma lies to the south. The Missouri River makes a jagged notch along the state's northeast border.

Kansas Cities

NEBRASKA

COLORADO

Missouri River

Oakley •

Minneapolis •

• Salina

Manhattan •

Topeka ⊛

Kansas City •

Lawrence •

Overland Park •

KANSAS

Garden City •

Hutchinson •

Dodge City •

Wichita •

MISSOURI

OKLAHOMA

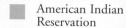

Legend

▪	American Indian Reservation
⊛	Capital
•	City
⌇	River

N
W   E
S

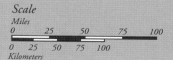

Scale
Miles
0   25   50   75   100

0   25   50   75   100
Kilometers

Kansas' flat prairie offers views of the sky in every direction.

Chapter 2

Land, Climate, and Wildlife

Kansas is a prairie state. The flat land is nearly treeless. Kansans enjoy views stretching to the horizon. Today, farmers have plowed most of the grassy prairie for farmland.

One of the flattest states, Kansas is not completely flat. The land slopes gradually up toward the west. The state is divided into three main land regions. They are the Great Plains, Dissected Till Plains, and Southeastern Plains.

The Great Plains

The Great Plains spread across central and western Kansas. The region is an open grassland that stretches across the

middle of North America from southern Canada to Texas. When the Ice Age ended, wind and streams from glaciers carried sand and other material to central North America. These deposits formed the Great Plains. The Arkansas River flows through the middle of the region on its way to the Mississippi River.

The western part of the Great Plains region is called the High Plains. This area of Kansas contains the state's highest point. Mount Sunflower is a hill rising 4,039 feet (1,231 meters) above sea level.

The Smoky Hills rise over the north-central area of the Great Plains. The Smoky Hill, Saline, and Solomon Rivers flow through the hills.

Dissected Till Plains

The Dissected Till Plains are in the northeastern corner of Kansas. The Big Blue River forms the region's western border. The Missouri River lies to the northeast. The Kansas River borders the region to the south.

Glaciers covered the Dissected Till Plains during the Ice Age. As the glaciers melted, they left behind clay, sand, and gravel. These deposits created rolling hills and rich soil called till. The rivers wore away the rock, forming high bluffs.

Kansas' Land Features

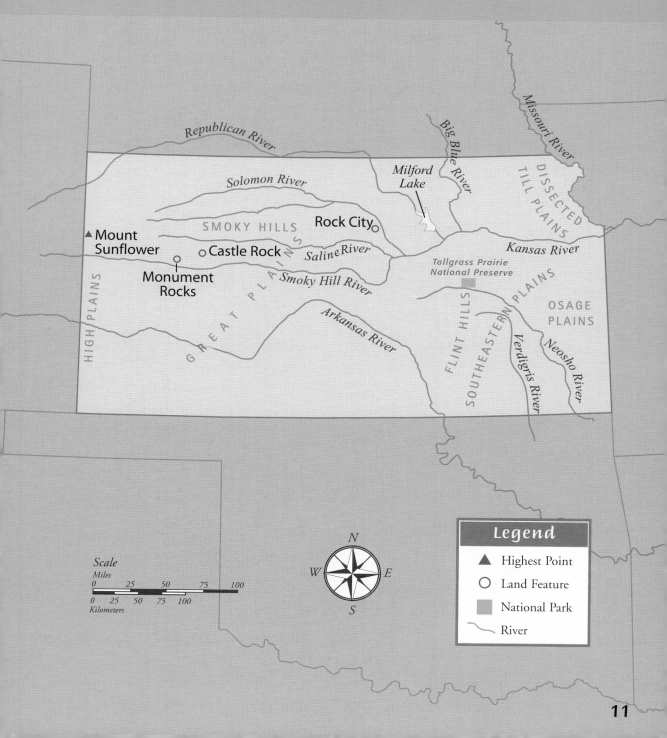

Republican River

Missouri River

Solomon River

Big Blue River

Milford Lake

DISSECTED TILL PLAINS

SMOKY HILLS

Rock City

▲ Mount Sunflower

○ Castle Rock

Saline River

Kansas River

Monument Rocks

Smoky Hill River

Tallgrass Prairie National Preserve

HIGH PLAINS

GREAT PLAINS

Arkansas River

FLINT HILLS

SOUTHEASTERN PLAINS

OSAGE PLAINS

Verdigris River

Neosho River

Scale
Miles
0   25   50   75   100
0   25   50   75   100
Kilometers

N
W   E
S

Legend
▲ Highest Point
○ Land Feature
■ National Park
〰 River

Southeastern Plains

The Southeastern Plains region is east of the Great Plains and south of the Dissected Till Plains. The Southeastern Plains region includes two smaller regions called the Osage Plains and the Flint Hills.

The Osage Plains form the eastern part of the Southeastern Plains. Shallow seas covered the plains about 245 million years ago. The sea filled and dried up several times as Earth's climate changed. Over millions of years, sandy material and bits of shells formed layers of limestone and shale rock. Later, wind and water wore away the rock to form steep cliffs called cuestas.

The Flint Hills lie west of the Osage Plains. The hard, rocky ground of the hills is difficult to plow. Farmers left this area alone, so some areas of prairie have been preserved. The Tallgrass Prairie National Preserve is one of the few areas of native prairie grassland left in the United States.

Climate

Kansas' weather changes widely between the seasons. During winter, cold northern air blows across the plains. The average temperature is 30 degrees Fahrenheit (minus 1 degree Celsius). Summers are hot and sunny, with an average

Near the Flint Hills, Tallgrass Prairie National Preserve is one of the few areas of native grassland in the United States.

The State Reptile

The ornate box turtle is Kansas' state reptile. Its name comes from the pattern of yellow markings on its brown or black shell.

Ornate box turtles are suited to life on the prairie. They eat insects, grass, and berries. In the winter, they dig into the ground to hibernate.

A sixth-grade class in Caldwell helped make the ornate box turtle the state reptile. The students wrote letters and visited the capitol in Topeka. They spread their message by newspapers and radio. The class watched as Governor John Carlin signed the Ornate Box Turtle Bill on April 14, 1986.

temperature of 77 degrees Fahrenheit (25 degrees Celsius). Southern Kansas is slightly warmer than northern Kansas.

An average of 27 inches (69 centimeters) of precipitation falls in the state each year. The most precipitation falls in the southeast. There, precipitation averages 35 inches (89 centimeters) each year. In contrast, the High Plains receive an average of only 19 inches (48 centimeters) of precipitation each year.

Storms

Many storms pass through Kansas. Some windstorms develop into tornadoes. Tornadoes' twisting winds can reach speeds of more than 300 miles (480 kilometers) per hour. Each year, an average of 39 tornadoes touch the ground in Kansas. The state's deadliest tornado struck the town of Udall on May 25, 1955. The storm killed 75 people and injured 270 others.

On May 25, 1955, a deadly tornado flattened much of Udall, Kansas.

Elk Falls is part of the Elk River in southeastern Kansas. Many types of fish live in Kansas' rivers and lakes.

Hailstorms occur in Kansas. Hard ice balls fall with enough force to dent metal, break windows, and flatten crops.

Weather in Kansas also brings droughts, dust storms, blizzards, and floods. The state's deadliest flood was in 1903. The Smoky Hill River flooded much of Salina, killing 415 people.

Plants and Wildlife

About 200 grasses grow in Kansas. In the High Plains, buffalo grass, sandreed, and salt grass grow well in the hot, dry summers. Big bluestem and other tall grasses grow throughout the state.

Prairies provide homes for small animals such as rabbits, gophers, and prairie dogs. Hawks, snakes, and other animals hunt these small animals.

Cheyenne Bottoms is a wetland near Great Bend in the center of the state. Millions of birds stop in this protected area when flying north in the spring.

Kansas' waters are home to many types of fish. Bass, walleye, and catfish swim through the state's rivers and lakes.

American Indians guided Francisco Vásquez de Coronado and his explorers across the Kansas plains in 1541.

Chapter 3

History of Kansas

In the 1500s, several American Indian tribes lived in Kansas. Some of these tribes had moved to Kansas from other parts of the country. Kansa Indians, also called Kaw, came to Kansas from the Atlantic coast. They settled in villages along the Missouri River in northeastern Kansas. The state is named after this tribe. The Osage lived near the Kansa in villages along the Neosho, Missouri, and Arkansas Rivers. The Pawnee and Wichita Indians lived along the Arkansas River. Other tribes hunted buffalo in western Kansas. These tribes were the Arapaho, Cheyenne, Kiowa, and Comanche.

European Explorers

In 1541, Francisco Vásquez de Coronado led Spanish explorers from Mexico to Kansas. Coronado's explorers traveled as far as a Wichita village along the Arkansas River.

Explorers from France arrived in the 1600s. They traded furs with the Pawnee and Osage Indians. The French claimed the land west of the Mississippi River for France. This area, which included Kansas, was called Louisiana. In 1803, President Thomas Jefferson bought Louisiana from France in the Louisiana Purchase.

U.S. Army Lieutenant Zebulon Pike explored what is now Kansas in 1806.

Jefferson wanted to know about the land and people west of the Mississippi River. He sent Meriwether Lewis and William Clark to explore the land. Lewis and Clark left St. Louis, Missouri, in May 1804. They traveled through northeastern Kansas along the Missouri River on their way to the Pacific Ocean. They completed their journey in September 1806.

Indian Removal Act

Other explorers followed Lewis and Clark. In 1806, the U.S. Army sent Zebulon Pike to Kansas to begin peaceful talks with American Indians. In 1819, Major Stephen Long also explored the area.

Most people did not know about the rich soil of the Great Plains. Few people wanted to settle in Kansas. Instead, they wanted to take Indian lands in the eastern United States. In 1830, Congress passed the Indian Removal Act. Because of this law, the Shawnee and other eastern tribes had to move to Kansas.

Crossroads of the West

Many settlers traveled west through Kansas by stagecoach and wagon. The 900-mile (1,448-kilometer) Santa Fe Trail opened in 1821. The trail cut across the center of Kansas along the Kansas and the Arkansas Rivers.

The Oregon Trail passed through the northeastern corner of Kansas. From 1841 to 1869, more than 500,000 people traveled this trail. It stretched more than 2,000 miles (3,200 kilometers) from Missouri to Oregon.

The Smoky Hill Trail began in 1862 as a mail route. The trail ran west from Atchison along part of the old Cherokee Trail. From 1862 until 1868, more than 20,000 settlers traveled this trail each year. After the Kansas Pacific Railroad was completed in 1869, few people ever used the trail again.

Statehood and a Civil War

As people traveled west, many wanted to settle in Kansas. In 1854, Congress passed the Kansas-Nebraska Act. This law allowed people to settle in Kansas Territory and Nebraska Territory.

The people of Kansas Territory wanted statehood. Under the rules of the Kansas-Nebraska Act, they had to choose whether they wanted to be a free or a slave state. In the mid-1800s, the United States had an equal number of free and slave states. People against slavery were called abolitionists.

Pawnee Rock was a landmark for people traveling along the Santa Fe Trail in Kansas. Many settlers camped near the rock. Today, it is a state historic site.

They moved to Kansas to support its entrance as a free state. People who supported slavery crossed into Kansas from the slave state of Missouri. They planned to vote illegally for Kansas to be a slave state.

John Brown and his sons were abolitionists who murdered five pro-slavery settlers at Pottawatomie Creek. In October 1859, Brown led an attack on a weapons storehouse at Harpers Ferry, Virginia. Local militiamen stopped Brown and his men. Brown was tried and sentenced to death. He was hanged on December 2.

Many settlers came to Kansas to claim free land after the U.S. Congress passed the Homestead Act in 1862.

"If I went west, I think I would go to Kansas."
—*Abraham Lincoln, 16th president of the United States*

As Kansas moved toward statehood, about 50 people were killed in the fight over slavery. Senator Charles Sumner of Massachusetts called the territory "bleeding Kansas." The abolitionists won the battle. On January 29, 1861, Kansas entered the Union as a free state. Topeka became its capital.

In 1860 and 1861, 11 Southern states left the United States. These states formed the Confederate States of America, known as the Confederacy. This action led to the Civil War (1861–1865). Most Kansas men served in the U.S. Army, but some Kansans helped the Confederacy. The Civil War ended in 1865 when the Confederacy surrendered. Slaves were freed after the war.

Settling Kansas

In 1862, the Homestead Act gave 160 acres (65 hectares) of free land in western states to each settler. Between 1862 and 1900, thousands of settlers moved to Kansas to claim land.

As more settlers came to Kansas, trouble began between settlers and American Indians. The U.S. Army built Fort Hays, Fort Dodge, Fort Wallace, and other posts to control the Indians. The government made many tribes give up their lands. The tribes also lost their main source of food as hunters killed most of the huge buffalo herds.

Cattle Drives

The prairie states were good places to raise cattle. Many cattle towns were founded in Kansas, including Abilene, Wichita, and Dodge City. From 1867 to 1875, cowboys drove huge herds of cattle from Texas to Kansas along the Chisholm Trail. The trail stretched 1,000 miles (1,600 kilometers), ending at the Abilene rail yards.

Trade soon became an important industry in Kansas. The Transcontinental Railroad made it possible to ship Kansas meat and leather to the eastern states. The railroad also brought settlers and goods from the eastern states to Kansas.

Early Farming

In 1874, a huge swarm of grasshoppers called locusts moved through the state. The hungry locusts ate entire fields of crops in a matter of hours.

The same year, a religious group came to Kansas from Russia. These Mennonites wanted to practice their religion freely. Each Mennonite family brought winter wheat seed called Turkey Red. This seed was planted in the fall. The wheat was harvested in early summer before insects or high temperatures could damage it. Turkey Red wheat grew well in Kansas. Mills were built to grind the wheat into flour. Kansas became known as the "breadbasket of the world."

Hard Times

In 1917, the United States entered World War I (1914–1918). Kansas farmers sent beef and wheat to feed soldiers fighting in

Huge cattle drives were common in Kansas beginning in the mid-1800s.

In May 1937, a dust storm hit Elkhart in southwestern Kansas.

Europe. Soldiers trained at Fort Leavenworth and Fort Riley. Kansas oil and gasoline powered army vehicles and machines. The state also supplied a lightweight gas called helium for the war effort. Helium is present in natural gas. The army used helium to fill aircraft called dirigibles. Soldiers used dirigibles to patrol areas where airplanes could not easily fly.

In 1929, the stock market crashed. This event was the beginning of the Great Depression (1929–1939). Many banks and companies went out of business. During the early years of the depression, Kansas did a little better than some states because of the importance of its wheat crops.

About 1931, a seven-year drought began in the Midwest. Lack of rain and high temperatures destroyed crops. The wind picked up the soil and carried it across the plains. The dust formed huge clouds that darkened the sky. The Great Plains soon became known as the dust bowl.

World War II

In 1941, the United States entered World War II (1939–1945). Preparing for war put companies back in business and ended the Great Depression. More than 25,000 Kansans found work in the state's aircraft plants.

Amelia Earhart

Kansas was home to one of the world's most famous pilots. Amelia Earhart was born in 1897 in Atchison, Kansas. She lived there until she was 11.

In 1922, Earhart earned her pilot's license and bought her first plane. In May 1932, she was the first woman to fly alone across the Atlantic Ocean. In January 1935, she was the first pilot to fly from Hawaii to California.

On June 1, 1937, Earhart began an attempt to fly around the world. On July 2, her airplane disappeared near Howland Island in the Pacific Ocean. Neither Earhart nor her plane has ever been found.

Dwight D. Eisenhower, who grew up in Abilene, commanded the Allied forces in Europe. After the war ended, Eisenhower was elected president of the United States in 1952 and again in 1956.

"The proudest thing I can say today is that I'm from Abilene."
—Dwight D. Eisenhower, 34th president of the United States

Recent Times

Kansas suffered its worst drought between 1952 and 1957. Many less severe droughts occurred between 1961 and 1972. Still, the state's wheat crops continued to do well. Irrigation systems brought underground water to the fields. Farmers planted trees between the fields and plowed the fields in patterns to prevent soil erosion. Scientists developed new varieties of wheat to grow in dry conditions.

Kansas grew more wheat than the United States could use. In 1972, the United States sold grain to the Soviet Union. This country later split to form Russia and several smaller countries. The Soviet Union bought 33 million tons (30 million metric tons) of wheat and corn. At that time, the sale was the largest trade deal ever made. The sale helped the Kansas economy.

Today, many Kansas farm workers have moved to the cities for new jobs. Many of these people work at the state's aviation and space equipment companies.

The Kansas Statehouse was completed in 1903 in Topeka.

Chapter 4

Government and Politics

Kansans have always had a strong voice in national politics. In the early 1860s, Kansans voted with the antislavery Republican Party. The state has supported mainly Republican presidential candidates. But since the 1950s, more Kansas governors have been Democrats than Republicans.

Several Kansans had a part in national politics. Dwight D. Eisenhower was the nation's 34th president. Former Kansas Governor Alf Landon was the Republican candidate for president in 1936. He lost to Franklin D. Roosevelt. Sixty years later, Kansas Senator Bob Dole ran for president as a Republican. He lost to Bill Clinton.

State Constitution

During the 1850s, Kansans faced the challenge of writing a state constitution. Kansans had to decide the territory's position on slavery. They could then approve a constitution and apply for statehood.

As they wrote their set of laws, Kansas lawmakers used Ohio's constitution as a guide. On July 5, 1859, delegates met at Wyandotte to sign the document. The state still uses the same constitution, but it has been changed many times.

Branches of Government

Kansas' government is divided into three areas. These areas are the executive, legislative, and judicial branches.

The governor is the leader of the executive branch. The governor is elected to a four-year term. The governor can be elected to an unlimited number of terms. Governors can serve no more than two terms in a row.

A senate and a house of representatives form the legislative branch. The 40 state senators are elected to four-year terms. The 125 representatives serve two-year terms.

Kansas' State Government

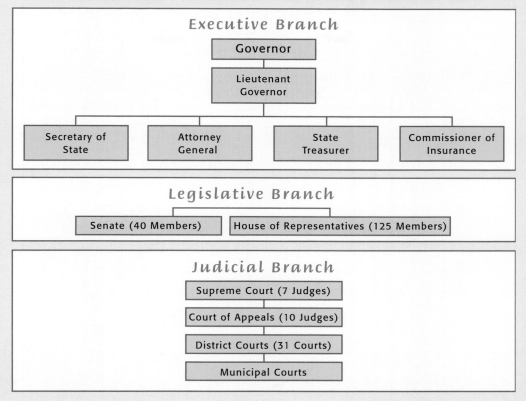

Executive Branch

- Governor
  - Lieutenant Governor
    - Secretary of State
    - Attorney General
    - State Treasurer
    - Commissioner of Insurance

Legislative Branch

- Senate (40 Members)
- House of Representatives (125 Members)

Judicial Branch

- Supreme Court (7 Judges)
- Court of Appeals (10 Judges)
- District Courts (31 Courts)
- Municipal Courts

The state judicial branch includes municipal courts, district courts, the Kansas Court of Appeals, and the Kansas Supreme Court. Municipal courts hear cases dealing with local laws. District courts serve one or more counties. Most criminal trials are heard in district courts. The Kansas Court of Appeals handles appeals from other courts. The Kansas Supreme Court makes final decisions about cases first heard in other state courts.

Reforms and Civil Rights

In the 1880s, Kansas farmers and ranchers formed the Farmers' Alliance. This group supported lower railroad shipping fees for grain and lower interest rates from banks. By the 1890s, the Alliance was part of a national political party called the People's Party. Many people called it the Populist Party. Kansans elected many Populist state officials, including two governors and a U.S. senator. The party's power decreased by the end of the 1890s. Still, its victories showed Kansans they could work together to improve their state.

In 1912, Kansas legislators passed a law that gave the right to vote to Kansas women. These suffrage supporters are shown at a camp near Winfield, Kansas, in 1910.

Kansans have continued to work for other improvements. In 1912, Kansas was the eighth state to give women the right to vote in state elections. Kansas also outlawed child labor and set up courts for young people accused of crimes.

During the 1950s, Kansas struggled with civil rights issues, along with the rest of the country. African Americans did not receive the same rights and treatment as white citizens. African Americans often were forced to go to separate, or segregated, schools. Most of the segregated schools were crowded and lacked basic supplies.

One of the most important civil rights court cases was filed in Kansas. In 1951, the father of 8-year-old Linda Brown sued the Topeka School Board. The suit came about when Linda was not allowed to attend an all-white school near her home. *Brown v. Board of Education of Topeka* went to the U.S. Supreme Court. In 1954, the Supreme Court ruled that school segregation was against the U.S. Constitution. Schools across the country were then required to admit students of all races.

Recent Events

Kansas has continued its history of improvement. In 1980, the state became the first to set up programs to stop child abuse. In 1990, Kansas elected its first woman governor, Joan Finney.

A machine called a combine harvests wheat in a Kansas field. Kansas is the top producer of wheat in the United States.

Chapter 5

Economy and Resources

Kansas is a leading agricultural state, but it does not depend on farming alone. Manufacturing and service industries provide most jobs in Kansas.

Agriculture

Farmland covers nearly 90 percent of Kansas. All of this land is farmed by fewer than 10 percent of Kansas workers. In recent years, large corporate farms have replaced many small family farms.

Beef cattle and wheat make the most money for Kansas farmers. Beef cattle make up 60 percent of farm earnings. Wheat provides 13 percent, but Kansas still produces more wheat than any other state. Nearly 10 million acres (4 million hectares) of the state's land is used to grow wheat. Nearly all of the wheat raised in Kansas is winter wheat.

Kansas farmers raise other crops. Sorghum is used as livestock feed or is made into molasses. Farmers also raise corn, soybeans, and sunflowers.

Manufacturing

Kansas leads the nation in manufacturing aircraft. Manufacturers with plants in Wichita include Boeing, Cessna, Raytheon, and Bombardier/Learjet.

Several aircraft research companies are located in Kansas. Some of these companies work with the space program. Kansas engineers designed the breathing systems used on Apollo space flights and on the space shuttle.

Food processing is another important Kansas industry. Meatpacking plants process beef. Mills grind wheat into flour.

Mining

Many kinds of rock are mined in Kansas and used for building materials. Limestone mined in eastern Kansas is cut into blocks for buildings or crushed to use in cement. Sand

Kansas aircraft plants make Boeing jets in Wichita. The city is known as the "air capital of the world."

Each month, Kansas oil wells produce a total of about 2 million barrels of oil.

mined near rivers is melted for glass. Clay and shale from central and eastern Kansas are used to make pottery, ceramics, tile, and bricks. Gypsum is mined in north-central Kansas. It is used to make wallboard and plaster.

Salt mining is a major industry in central Kansas. In 1887, people drilling for oil near Hutchinson discovered salt. The salt was left when a prehistoric ocean dried up. Much of the salt is mined in large caves about 650 feet (200 meters) underground.

Oil and natural gas are other important resources. Oil was found in Kansas in 1860. The state's first large oil well began producing in 1893 near Neodesha. Natural gas was discovered in 1873. The Hugoton Gas Field is the largest natural gas field in the country. It runs beneath 10 of Kansas' southwestern counties and into Oklahoma.

Service Industries

Most jobs in Kansas are in service industries. Government workers, teachers, retail clerks, bankers, and insurance agents are all service workers.

Many large service companies began in Kansas. Cleyson Brown started the Brown Telephone Company in Abilene in 1899. The company changed its name to Sprint in 1992. Today, Sprint serves 23 million customers in 70 countries.

In 1958, brothers Frank and Dan Carney borrowed $600 from their mother and started Pizza Hut. They began their business in a small building in Wichita. Today, the company has 12,000 restaurants that employ about 300,000 workers in 89 countries.

Fort Leavenworth has served the U.S. Army since 1827. Today, Fort Leavenworth is home to the Combined Arms Center. This school trains U.S. Army officers for battle.

Big Brutus

The world's second largest electric shovel is on display in West Mineral. "Big Brutus" is 160 feet (49 meters) tall and weighs 11 million pounds (5 million kilograms).

From 1963 to 1974, Big Brutus was used to dig large coal pits. Today, the shovel is a museum. Visitors can walk inside the shovel to its top.

Military

For many years, Kansas' central location has been important to the U.S. military. Built in 1827, Fort Leavenworth is the oldest army post west of the Mississippi River still in operation. The military's largest prison is at Fort Leavenworth.

Kansas is home to other important military sites. The army built Fort Riley near Manhattan in 1853. McConnell Air Force Base is near Wichita.

Festivals in Kansas, such as this chili cook-off in Lenexa, celebrate the state's heritage, culture, and ethnic backgrounds.

Chapter 6

People and Culture

Kansas is a growing state. Its population of 2,688,418 ranks 32nd among the states. Kansas' population increased 8.5 percent from 1990 to 2000.

Much daily life in Kansas still revolves around ranching and farming. But the varied ethnic backgrounds of its residents and the energy of its large cities also influence the state's culture.

The People

Kansans have many ethnic backgrounds. Most Kansans descended from European immigrants. These people came to the United States in the 1800s from Germany, Russia, England, France, Sweden, and other European countries.

During the early 1900s, many people moved to Kansas from Mexico. Today, Garden City and Dodge City in western Kansas have large Hispanic populations.

About 50,000 African Americans moved to Kansas from the South after the Civil War. These people were known as Exodusters. They started African American towns such as Nicodemus. This town still exists today.

Asian Americans make up less than 2 percent of Kansas' population. Many moved to Kansas from Southeast Asia in the 1970s and 1980s.

At one time, American Indians lived throughout Kansas. Today, members of the Potawatomi, Iowa, Sac and Fox, and

In 1995, crop artist Stan Herd created this picture of the Statue of Liberty in a field near Lawrence, Kansas.

Kansas' Ethnic Background

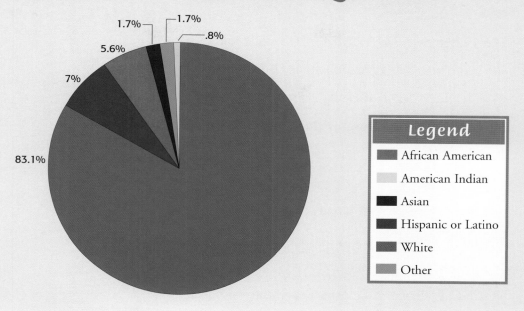

1.7%
1.7%
.8%
5.6%
7%
83.1%

Legend
- African American
- American Indian
- Asian
- Hispanic or Latino
- White
- Other

Kickapoo tribes live in Kansas. Some tribe members live on reservations located in the northeastern part of the state.

Artists and Writers

Many talented artists come from Kansas. John Steuart Curry grew up in Kansas during the early 1900s. Curry painted murals for the Kansas Statehouse in Topeka. His murals also are found in government buildings in Washington, D.C.

Stan Herd creates pictures in fields using different crops and ways of plowing. His work is best seen from airplanes.

The Wizard of Oz

The 1939 movie *The Wizard of Oz* made Kansas famous. The movie is based on the book *The Wonderful Wizard of Oz* by L. Frank Baum. In the movie, a girl named Dorothy Gale longs to leave her Kansas farm. A tornado carries Dorothy away to the colorful land of Oz. She spends the rest of the movie trying to get home to her family and friends in Kansas.

In Liberal, people can see objects from the movie at the Land of Oz Museum. The town has a paved yellow brick road and a replica of Dorothy's house. Each October, the town hosts a festival called Oztoberfest.

Several well-known African American writers have roots in Kansas. Beginning in the 1920s, Langston Hughes wrote poems, novels, and plays about matters important to African Americans. Gordon Parks was born in Fort Scott. He is a well-known writer, photographer, composer, and film director. In 1950, poet Gwendolyn Brooks, who was born in Topeka, became the first African American to win a Pulitzer Prize.

Other Pulitzer Prize-winning writers lived in Kansas. Emporia newspaper editor William Allen White won Pulitzer Prizes in 1923 and 1947. In 1953, William Inge won a Pulitzer Prize for his play *Picnic*. The play is set in Inge's hometown of Independence.

Music

Kansas has produced talented musicians. During the 1940s and 1950s, Kansas City native Charlie Parker played the saxophone and wrote songs in a form of jazz called bebop. Coffeyville native Eva Jessye was a well-known singer, poet, and composer. The rock band "Kansas" formed in Topeka in the early 1970s and recorded many hit songs in the 1970s and 1980s.

Festivals and concerts celebrate the many musical talents and backgrounds within the state. Each April, the Wichita Jazz Festival attracts top jazz musicians from around the country. In September, bluegrass fans gather in Winfield for the Walnut Valley Festival. A choir in Lindsborg has performed Handel's *Messiah* each Easter season since 1880.

Food and Festivals

Kansans enjoy many types of food. Kansas is known for its barbecue recipes. Cooks brush spicy tomato sauces onto ribs, steaks, and hamburgers. Living in the "world's breadbasket," Kansas bakers make many types of breads and other baked goods.

Other events and festivals feature culture and the arts. Each May, the Wichita River Festival includes outdoor concerts, hot-air balloon rides, and fireworks. Summer powwows celebrate American Indian culture. People enjoy traditional games, food, dances, and music. Fiesta Mexicana takes place in Topeka each July. This Mexican American festival includes dances, a parade, games, and traditional food

and music. Each fall, the Renaissance Festival is a popular event in Bonner Springs. Visitors find shows, costumes, crafts, and games from medieval England.

Reform for the Future

Kansas was settled by farmers and ranchers. Today, this prairie state is known for much more than wheat and beef. Throughout the state's history, Kansans have fought for their rights and beliefs. They have worked together to make life better for people in their state and the country as a whole.

Wichita is home to the Wichita River Festival, which celebrates the city's connection to the Arkansas River.

Recipe: Granola

This sweet, crunchy treat includes many ingredients produced in Kansas.

Ingredients

3 cups (720 mL) oats (not instant)
1 cup (240 mL) wheat germ
1 cup (240 mL) sunflower kernels
½ cup (120 mL) brown sugar
1 teaspoon (5 mL) salt
⅓ cup (80 mL) sunflower oil or
    canola oil
½ cup (120 mL) molasses
1 tablespoon (15 mL) vanilla

Equipment

dry-ingredient measuring cups
measuring spoons
liquid measuring cups
large bowl
small bowl
mixing spoons
large baking sheet
nonstick cooking spray
oven mitts
spatula

What You Do

1. Preheat oven to 350°F (180°C).

2. Mix oats, wheat germ, sunflower kernels, brown sugar, and salt in large bowl.

3. In small bowl, mix sunflower oil or canola oil, molasses, and vanilla.

4. Pour molasses mixture over oats mixture. Mix together so that oats mixture is completely coated.

5. Spray baking sheet with nonstick cooking spray.

6. Spread granola mixture onto baking sheet.

7. Bake for 15 minutes or until golden brown. While granola is baking, use oven mitts to remove baking sheet every 5 minutes and stir the mixture with a mixing spoon.

8. Remove pan from oven and allow granola to cool for one-half hour.

9. Remove granola from baking sheet with spatula. Eat as a snack or with milk as cereal.

Makes about 8 cups

Kansas' Flag and Seal

Kansas Flag

The state flag is royal blue, with the state's name at the bottom and the state seal in the center. Above the seal, a sunflower represents Kansas' nickname, the Sunflower State.

Kansas State Seal

The Kansas state seal has images that show the state's history. The seal includes a rising sun, a farmer plowing a field, and wagons heading west. Other images on the seal are a herd of buffalo, two American Indians, and a steamboat traveling on a river. The Kansas state motto is at the top. "Ad astra per aspera" means, "To the stars through difficulties." Underneath the motto, 34 stars represent Kansas' position as the 34th state.

Almanac

Nickname: Sunflower State

Population: 2,688,418 (U.S. Census, 2000)
Population rank: 32nd

Capital: Topeka

Largest cities: Wichita, Kansas City, Topeka, Overland Park, Lawrence

Area: 82,282 square miles (213,110 square kilometers)
Size rank: 15th

Highest point: Mount Sunflower, 4,039 feet (1,231 meters) above sea level

Lowest point: Verdigris River, 680 feet (207 meters) above sea level

Agricultural products: Wheat, sorghum, corn, hay, soybeans, sunflowers, cattle, sheep

Average summer temperature: 77 degrees Fahrenheit (25 degrees Celsius)

Average winter temperature: 30 degrees Fahrenheit (minus 1 degree Celsius)

Average annual precipitation: 27 inches (69 centimeters)

bison

western meadowlark

Animal: American buffalo (bison)

Bird: Western meadowlark

Flower: Native sunflower

Insect: Honeybee

Reptile: Ornate box turtle

Song: "Home on the Range," by Dr. Brewster Higley

Tree: Cottonwood

Natural resources: Salt, crushed stone, helium, sand, gravel, natural gas, oil

Types of industry: Aircraft and machinery manufacturing, food processing, communications and computer equipment

First governor: Charles Robinson

Statehood: January 29, 1861; 34th state

U.S. Representatives: 4

U.S. Senators: 2

U.S. electoral votes: 6

Counties: 105

native sunflower

Timeline

State History

1500s
Kansa, Pawnee, Osage, and Wichita people are living in present-day Kansas when European explorers arrive.

1804–1819
Lewis and Clark, Zebulon Pike, and Stephen Long explore Kansas.

1854
The Kansas-Nebraska Act creates the Kansas Territory.

1861
Kansas becomes the 34th state on January 29.

1874
Mennonites bring Turkey Red wheat to Kansas.

U.S. History

1620
Pilgrims establish a colony in the New World.

1775–1783
American colonists and the British fight the Revolutionary War.

1861–1865
The Union and the Confederacy fight the Civil War.

1954
The U.S. Supreme Court rules against school segregation in *Brown v. Board of Education of Topeka.*

1931–1938
Kansas and much of the Midwest experience a severe drought; the area is called the dust bowl.

2000s
Kansas is a leader in the aircraft manufacturing industry.

1952
Kansas native Dwight D. Eisenhower is elected the 34th President.

1912
Kansas women win the right to vote.

1972
Much of Kansas' wheat crop is part of a large sale to the Soviet Union.

1939–1945
World War II is fought; the United States enters the war in 1941.

2001
On September 11, terrorists attack the World Trade Center and the Pentagon.

1914–1918
World War I is fought; the United States enters the war in 1917.

1929–1939
The United States experiences the Great Depression.

1964
U.S. Congress passes the Civil Rights Act, which makes any form of discrimination illegal.

Words to Know

abolitionist (ab-uh-LISH-uh-nist)—a person opposed to slavery

aviation (ay-vee-AY-shuhn)—the science of building and flying aircraft

cuesta (KWESS-tuh)—a hill or ridge with a steep face on one side and a gentle slope on the other

drought (DROUT)—a long period of hot, dry weather

erosion (ih-ROH-zhuhn)—the gradual wearing away of land by water or wind

glacier (GLAY-shur)—a large sheet of slow-moving ice

helium (HEE-lee-uhm)—a lightweight, colorless gas that does not burn

immigrant (IM-uh-gruhnt)—a person who comes to another country to live permanently

irrigation (ihr-uh-GAY-shuhn)—to supply water to crops through ditches, pipes, or streams

prairie (PRAIR-ee)—a large area of flat, grassy land with few or no trees

segregation (seg-ruh-GAY-shuhn)—the practice of keeping people or groups apart

To Learn More

Bjorklund, Ruth. *Kansas*. Celebrate the States. New York: Benchmark Books, 2000.

Kummer, Patricia. *Kansas*. One Nation. Mankato, Minn.: Capstone Press, 2003.

Robinson Masters, Nancy. *Kansas*. America the Beautiful. New York: Children's Press, 1999.

Rosenthal, Marilyn, and Daniel Freeman. *Amelia Earhart*. Photo-Illustrated Biographies. Mankato, Minn.: Bridgestone Books, 1999.

Internet Sites

Track down many sites about Kansas.
Visit the FACT HOUND at *http://www.facthound.com*

IT IS EASY! IT IS FUN!
1) Go to *http://www.facthound.com*
2) Type in: 0736815848
3) Click on "FETCH IT" and FACT HOUND will find several links hand-picked by our editors.

Relax and let our pal FACT HOUND do the research for you!

Places to Write and Visit

Big Brutus Museum
P.O. Box 25
West Mineral, KS 66725

Kansas Cosmosphere and Space Center
1100 North Plum
Hutchinson, KS 67501

Kansas Department of Travel and Tourism
700 SW Harrison, Suite 1300
Topeka, KS 66603

Kansas State Historical Society
6425 SW Sixth Avenue
Topeka, KS 66615-1099

Kansas State Library
300 SW Tenth Avenue, Room 343-N
Topeka, KS 66612-1593

Land of Oz Museum
567 Yellow Brick Road
Liberal, KS 67901

Mushroom Rock is one of the unusual rock forms in Mushroom Rock State Park near Brookville.

Index

T 57072

West Union School
23870 NW West Union Road
Hillsboro, Oregon 97124